Health surveillance at work

HSE BOOKS

This guidance is issued by the Health and Safety Executive. Following the guidance is not compulsory and you are free to take other action. But if you do follow the guidance you will normally be doing enough to comply with the law. Health and safety inspectors seek to secure compliance with the law and may refer to this guidance as illustrating good practice.

Contents

HEALTH SURVEILLANCE

iv

Health surveillance at work

Introduction

1   Each year, many thousands of people become ill because of the work they do. Some suffer from diseases or conditions that can mean years of pain. Business loses billions of pounds through sickness absence and lost production.* Yet occupational ill health is preventable and many of these costs can be reduced by managers taking effective steps to control health risks at work. One of these steps is to arrange for the health surveillance of employees.

2   This guidance gives advice on what you need to do to meet your legal duty to provide health surveillance at work.   It outlines the health surveillance requirements of certain regulations, principally the Management of Health and Safety at Work Regulations 1992 (MHSW Regs) and the Control of Substances Hazardous to Health Regulations 1999 (COSHH). The guidance is directed mainly at those in charge of managing health risks at work but may interest safety representatives, workers and others involved with health surveillance programmes and those with existing programmes to ensure they remain on track.

3   The guidance:

- begins by describing health surveillance as it applies under health and safety regulations and how this is different from other measures to monitor employee health;

- lists some reasons why it is in your, and your employees' interests to carry out health surveillance;

- gives advice on the considerations you should take into account when assessing whether to introduce health surveillance;

- runs through the principles of carrying out effective health surveillance programmes and outlines good practice in doing so;

- gives advice on keeping and using health surveillance records; and

- signposts the way to other HSE publications for more information on health surveillance relating to particular hazards or sectors of industry; and to other sources of advice.

The 'risk assessment and action guide' on pages 2 - 3 summarises the action to follow when introducing health surveillance into your firm.

---

* Some 2 million individuals reported in 1995 that they suffered from illness caused or made worse by work (*Self-reported work-related illness in 1995,* 1998 HSE Books). The cost of work-related sickness was estimated at £11 billion in 1997 (CBI absence survey *Missing out* CBI 1998)

Health surveillance: Risk assessment and action guide

This risk assessment and action guide is here to help in deciding what you should ask yourself and what you need to do.

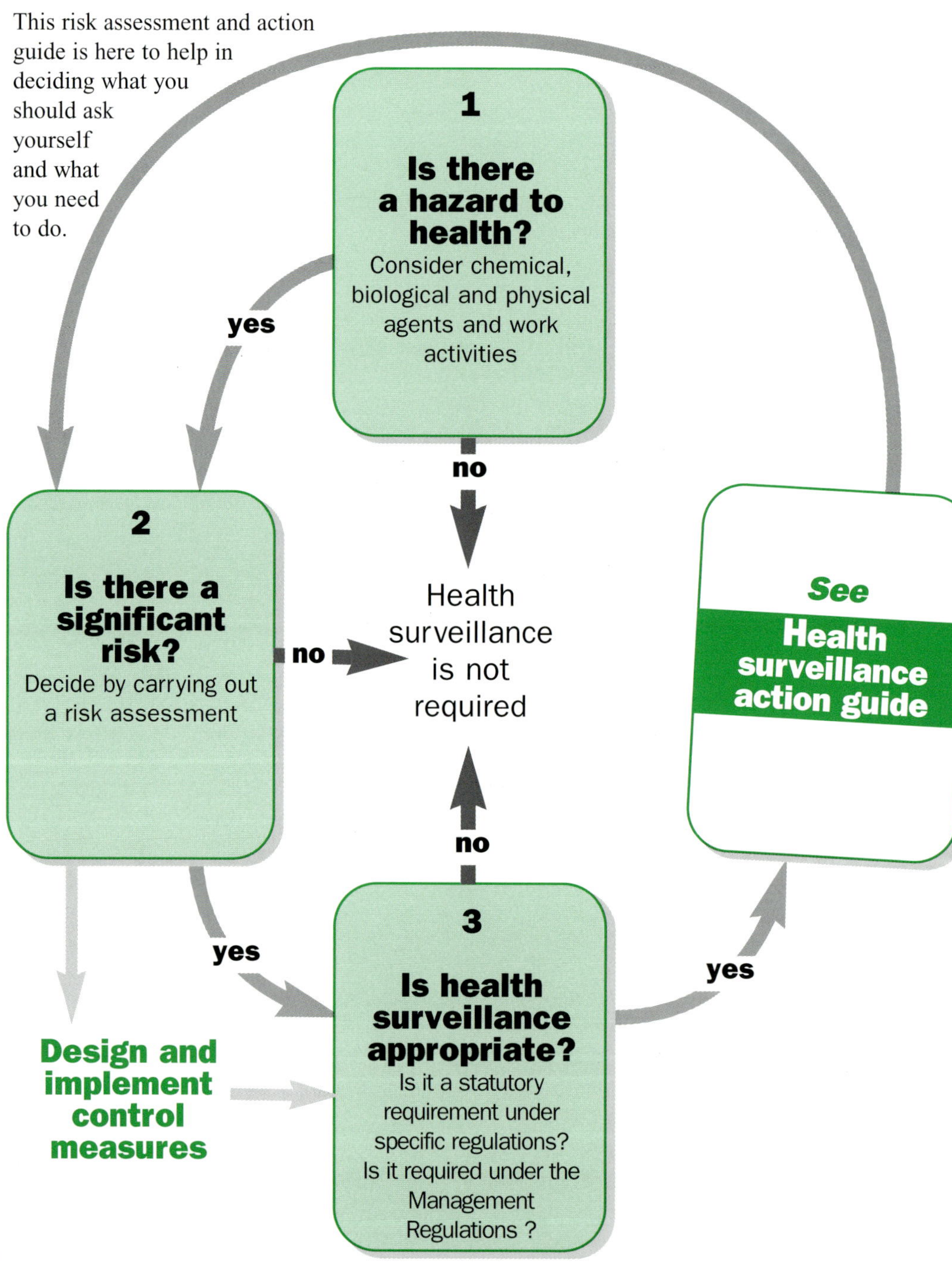

1 Involve employees and their representatives ☐

2 Obtain specialist advice if appropriate ☐

3 Identify the most suitable health surveillance procedure ☐

Consider the type of hazard, degree of risk, likely health effects, affected employees, relevant procedure(s), whether in-house expertise exists

4 Design system, put someone in charge ☐

5 Set up the programme

6 Carry out procedures/ feedback information ☐

7 Keep records ☐

8 Monitoring, action and evaluation ☐

Protect individuals at risk

Review your risk assessment

Improve risk control

Discuss grouped results with employee representatives

HEALTH SURVEILLANCE

What is health surveillance?

4   Health surveillance is about putting in place systematic, regular and appropriate procedures to detect early signs of work-related ill health among employees exposed to certain health risks; and acting on the results. To comply with the law, this means selecting from a range of specific techniques:

▶   *A 'responsible person' looking* for a clear reaction where someone is working with something that could harm their health. For example checking for skin damage on hands where solvents are being used, or checking answers on simple, periodic questionnaires about symptoms.

▶   *A 'qualified' person asking* employees about symptoms of ill health, or inspecting or examining individuals for signs of ill health. Examples might be someone conducting a hearing test, or an occupational health nurse carrying out a lung function test where workers regularly use certain paints.

▶   *Medical surveillance* by a doctor, which can include clinical examinations, for example to look for a reaction from exposure to some chemicals.

▶   *Biological and biological effect monitoring* to measure and assess the take-up of, or the effects of, exposure to substances such as lead or other chemicals, by testing blood, urine or breath samples.

▶   *Keeping individual health records* (see paragraphs 40-45).

5   Other elements of health surveillance include:

▶   *Self-checks by employees* to look for and report any signs of work-related ill health. These are an important part of any programme to pick up possible ill health effects. *However, self-checks on their own are not sufficient to comply with regulations.* They will help you to meet your duties only where they are part of a programme in which health records are kept and where employees are:

        - trained about what signs of disease or illness to look for and when and how to do so; and

        - told when and how to report any signs or symptoms to a responsible person or occupational health professional;

- also subject to periodic checks by someone else such as a responsible person.

▶ *Baseline health assessment*, carried out when a person takes up or changes job. This can be considered to be part of health surveillance only where it establishes baseline information that can be compared with the later results from surveillance. Always determine the need for such an assessment, and the way you carry it out, on the basis of its relevance to the job in question.

▶ *Giving information* to employees and their representatives and *referring employees* to an occupational health professional where extra checks are needed.

Other health monitoring procedures

There are other things you can do to monitor the health of your employees that should not be confused with health surveillance and so are beyond the scope of this document. Some may be legal duties, for example to assess fitness for work; others are not legal duties but can be used for other purposes, for example general annual health checks. The most common examples of legal duties are:

▶ Pre-placement and annual medical examinations to assess an individual's fitness for work, for example under the Ionising Radiations Regulations 1985 or under the Diving at Work Regulations 1997.

▶ Health screening to meet legal requirements, such as making eyesight testing available under the Health and Safety (Display Screen Equipment) Regulations 1992, or an assessment of someone's fitness to drive or operate cranes within dock premises (Docks Regulations 1988).

▶ Fitness for work health assessments offered to night workers under the Working Time Regulations 1998.

(You should also remember that under section 2 of the Health and Safety at Work etc Act 1974 (HSW) you have a general duty to ensure, so far as is reasonably practicable, the health, safety and welfare of all of your employees.)

The most common examples with no legal duty are:

▶ General non-statutory pre-employment health enquiries to check an individual's health status and medical history.

▶ Monitoring sickness absence records. These can be a useful source of intelligence and a means of assessing risk where more formal health surveillance procedures are not appropriate (see paragraph 11). Looking at collective sickness records could help you identify where there is a general problem affecting workers' health. Individual sickness records might indicate whether work is affecting an individual's health.

▶ Lifestyle health promotion and education to explain the benefits of, for example, enjoying a healthy diet, taking regular exercise, drinking sensibly and stopping smoking. This might be extended to include screening clinics, for example to test cholesterol and blood pressure levels. These activities are usually part of a benefits package, one purpose of which may be to reduce sickness absence.

▶ Annual health checks of key personnel. These can be extended to 'health MOTs' for all employees and may also help to assess the impact of health education at work.

▶ General testing of workers for evidence of drug or alcohol misuse, unless there are specific safety-critical implications.

HEALTH SURVEILLANCE

HEALTH SURVEILLANCE

Why carry out health surveillance?

6 The benefits of health surveillance are that it can:

▶ provide information so you can detect harmful health effects at an early stage, thereby protecting employees and confirming whether they are still fit to do their jobs;

▶ check that control measures are working well by giving feedback on risk assessments, suggesting where further action might be needed and what it might be;

▶ provide data, by means of the health records, to detect and evaluate health risks;

▶ provide an opportunity to train and instruct employees further in safe and healthy working practices, for example how to use personal protective equipment (PPE) properly; and

▶ give employees the chance to raise any concerns about the effect of their work on their health.

HEALTH SURVEILLANCE

Health Surveillance at work

When is health surveillance appropriate?

7   Don't think of health surveillance in isolation; it is one part of the overall management of health risks. Before introducing health surveillance:

▶ find out what the health hazards are where you work;

▶ identify those employees who might be at risk from being exposed to the hazards;

▶ decide what to do to make sure your employees' health is not harmed. To do this, try to get rid of the risk altogether. Where this cannot be done, see whether the risk can be reduced or controlled to such a level that it will not be harmful to health. This will not always be possible, so you will need to take further steps, such as providing PPE and introducing health surveillance.

8   Health surveillance is required where you answer 'yes' to *all* the following:

▶ Is the work known to damage health in some particular way?

▶ Are there valid ways to detect the disease or condition?* Health surveillance is only worthwhile where it can reliably show that damage to health is starting to happen or becoming likely. A technique is only useful if it provides accurate results, is safe and practical.

▶ Is it reasonably likely that damage to health may occur under the particular conditions at work?

▶ Is surveillance likely to benefit the employee?

9   For example, these criteria would be met in the following circumstances: High noise levels are known to cause hearing loss. A valid technique - hearing tests - can detect the effect of noise on the hearing of individuals who work in noisy conditions. Hearing tests will benefit employees by identifying those at risk so that measures can be taken to protect them and improve working conditions.

---

* Valid techniques are those that are precise enough to detect something wrong that could be caused by exposure to a particular health risk; and which are safe and practicable in a workplace setting.

Assessing the need for health surveillance

10   Other tips for assessing whether health surveillance might be appropriate include:

▶   if you know of previous cases of work-related ill health in your workplace;

▶   where you rely on PPE, for example gloves or respirators, as an exposure control measure. Even with the closest supervision, there is no guarantee that PPE will be effective at all times;

▶   where there is evidence of ill health in jobs found in your industry. Such information could come from insurance claims, manufacturers' and suppliers' data, HSE and other guidance and from industry experience.

11   Ask yourself whether any of your employees is exposed to the following:

▶   Hazardous substances such as chemicals, solvents, fumes, dusts, gases and vapours, aerosols, biological agents (micro-organisms). If so, health surveillance may be needed under the Control of Substances Hazardous to Health Regulations 1999.

▶   Asbestos, lead, work in compressed air. If so, medical examinations may be needed under specific regulations.

▶   Noise, hand-arm vibration. If so, health surveillance may be needed under the Management of Health and Safety at Work Regulations 1992.

▶   Manual handling, work that might give rise to stress-related diseases, work-related upper limb disorders, whole body vibration, hot and cold working, non-ionising electromagnetic radiation. The duty to provide health surveillance is unlikely to apply at present. This is primarily because valid ways to detect ill health conditions associated with these hazards do not exist and/or the link between the work activity and the ill health effect is uncertain. Nevertheless, use other procedures, for example symptom reporting by employees and checking sickness absence records, to ensure that you pick up possible ill health among your employees as early as possible so you can meet your duties under the HSW Act.

12   Health surveillance is not required where you are sure that there is no exposure or where the exposures that do take place are so rare, short and slight that there is only minimal risk of the employee being harmed. However, some substances can cause very serious illness such as cancers and for these there is often no level of exposure that can be regarded as completely safe. In these cases, health surveillance will almost always be required but may be limited to keeping health records.

13   See Appendix 1 for a list of HSE publications you may need to check to find out more about health surveillance. Many of these include guidance on which jobs might involve harmful exposures, the possible ill health effects and minimum health surveillance requirements.

14   In assessing the need for health surveillance, remember that:

▶   health surveillance is not a substitute for preventing or controlling harmful exposure to hazards, but a further way of seeking to protect employees' health;

▶   using the right technique, in the right way, at the right time is important. Getting it wrong can be expensive. Also bear in mind that some tests in themselves are not free from risk (eg X-rays) and the results, if inaccurate or not explained properly, could make employees worry unnecessarily;

▶   whichever technique is used, you should carry out health surveillance systematically and regularly; and

▶   simply carrying out health surveillance procedures is not enough; *it is essential that you act on the results.*

HEALTH SURVEILLANCE

Making health surveillance work

15   Ensure the success of your health surveillance programme by:

▶   being sure about its purpose;

▶   involving employees and their representatives and building trust;

▶   getting the programme right for your needs;

▶   being clear about roles and responsibilities;

▶   recording and acting on the results;

▶   dealing with special cases;

▶   monitoring, evaluating and, where appropriate, refining the programme.

The aim of the programme

16   Establish from the beginning the main purpose of your health
surveillance programme. Consider if its aim is simply to protect those workers
at risk from significant exposure to harmful agents and so meet your legal
duties; whether to extend the programme to all workers, irrespective of risk; or
if you also want to use it as a vehicle to put across messages about how people
can look after their own health, at work and at home.

17   Although only the courts can give an authoritative interpretation of the
law, in considering the application of regulations and guidance to persons
working under your direction, you should consider the following:

If you have people working under your control and direction who are treated as
self-employed for tax and NI purposes, they may nevertheless be treated as your
employees for health and safety purposes. You may therefore need to take
appropriate action to protect them. If you are in any doubt about who is
responsible for the health and safety of a person working for you this could be
clarified and included in the terms of the contract. However, remember, you
cannot pass on a legal duty that falls to you under the Health and Safety at
Work Act (HWSA) by means of a contract and you will still retain duties
towards others by virtue of section 3 of HSWA. If you intend to employ such
workers on the basis that you are not responsible for their health and safety, you
should seek legal advice before doing so.

18   Think about who to put in charge of, and be accountable for the programme, to ensure that it is introduced correctly, drawing on appropriate help; that it delivers the right results - for both you and your employees; and that information arising from it is being used to best effect.

Involving employees and their representatives

19   Health surveillance can fail where employees have not been told what its purpose is, how it will be carried out and what it means for them as individuals. Employees might suspect that programmes are introduced, not to protect them, but as a threat to their jobs.   Overcome this by involving employees, and, where appropriate, their representatives, early on. Where trade unions are recognised, consult safety representatives in good time about the development of any programme, covering the following issues:

▶   the aim of the programme, how it fits with your health and safety policy and other means you use to protect employees, and whether it is required by law;

▶   how employees can raise health and safety issues;

▶   the benefit to the individual in taking part, especially that it is not in their long-term health interests to conceal symptoms;

▶   what is involved, including any referral procedures;

▶   what information will be given to the employer, how this will be conveyed and what will happen with the results, including employment consequences;

▶   confidentiality; and

▶   how the programme will be monitored and evaluated.

20   Some health surveillance programmes involve clinical examinations and may include measurements of body fluids (or breath). Where this happens, it is essential that individual rights are protected and that employees understand and agree to the tests. In some cases, employees' written consent will be required. Such programmes should normally be under the supervision of a doctor with experience in occupational health.

21   Equally, employees should co-operate with you so that you can meet your health and safety duties under the law. Encourage employees to take part

positively in your health surveillance programme, explaining its importance and relevance to them. Ask them to report symptoms of ill health as soon as they notice them so that you can take prompt action to prevent further harm.

Introducing the right programme

22   You may well need to seek the advice of an occupational health professional to help you decide which type of health surveillance programme would best suit your needs. You may have to use a variety of different techniques, depending on the type and range of working practices and processes. The health professional will be able to help tailor your requirements to the type of business you run. However, this does not necessarily mean that doctors have to be directly involved in carrying out procedures; their role may often be more supervisory or to give advice.

WHO CAN CARRY OUT HEALTH SURVEILLANCE?

Roles and responsibilties

23   The duty to provide health surveillance under health and safety law rests with the employer, so you should therefore seek suitable outside help if there is none available within your firm. It is essential that people who carry out health surveillance are competent to do so. The level of competence depends on the tasks they have to perform. Choose someone who understands the aims of health surveillance and its procedures, who can advise you on the significance of the results and on how and when referral to a specialist might be necessary. Make sure that you are clear about what you expect from your adviser and what you can offer in return. As a guide, the table on page 18 shows where responsibility falls for certain procedures.

Responsible people

24   Responsible people need to be:

▶   carefully selected, ie they should be aware and have experience of the working environment and be able to gain the confidence and co-operation of employees and encourage good working methods;

▶   trained by an occupational health professional to be able to recognise and record specific signs (objective evidence of ill health) or symptoms (subjective indicators of ill health) that may be related to occupational exposure. Specific qualifications are not necessary;

Procedure	Who can do it?
Self-checks	Those exposed to hazards who have been properly trained in how to look for easily recognisable signs and symptoms of disease. They should know who to go to if they find anything that causes them concern. An example would be where employees notice sore, red and itching skin and who work with substances that cause skin damage. Note that such *self-checks on their own are not sufficient to comply with the Regulations* and can only be done as part of your overall health surveillance programme (see paragraph 5), for example where they complement checks by a responsible person.
A responsible person making basic checks for signs of disease	Anyone trained to identify straightforward signs and symptoms caused by working with certain substances or processes. Examples are skin inspections where people work with detergents, metalworking fluids or shampoos. Managers, supervisors or first aiders could carry out these checks. An occupational health doctor or nurse should train these people to recognise signs or symptoms requiring further assessment and to know when and how to refer employees. A responsible person must not be expected to diagnose the possible cause of symptoms.
Enquiries about symptoms, inspection and examination by a qualified person	Usually an occupational health nurse checking, for example, for signs of asthma; or someone with technical knowledge, for example an audiologist carrying out hearing tests or someone trained to conduct lung function tests.
Clinical examinations	Should be carried out by or be supervised by a doctor. In some cases this is a legal duty (for example for employees exposed to lead); in others the nature of the tests will require the expertise of a doctor to interpret the results and advise on their significance. Examination by a doctor is also likely to be necessary where health surveillance by a responsible person or an occupational health nurse has identified possible work-related ill health that requires further investigation, diagnosis and treatment.
Biological monitoring and biological effect monitoring	In general, these should be carried out by or supervised by a doctor. Some examples are tests for lead, mercury and carbon monoxide in blood; and cadmium and fluoride in urine. However in some circumstances, the actual taking of samples can be straightforward and be carried out by a suitably trained person.

▶ given clear instructions covering, for example, the methods to be used, the importance of confidentiality and the criteria for referring findings to the health care professional and reporting results of surveillance to you. Responsible people do not have to be medically qualified so they must not try to make judgements about the cause of symptoms.

Role of medical inspectors/appointed doctors

25   Some *medical* surveillance has to be undertaken by HSE medical inspectors or, more usually, by doctors appointed by HSE, for example where workers are exposed to lead, asbestos, ionising radiation, working in compressed air or with certain chemicals.   Such appointments allow HSE to monitor standards and collect statistics. An appointed doctor has a contractual responsibility to the employer of the person under surveillance as well as to HSE. In practice, this usually means confirming whether an employee remains fit to work with the agent or substance in question and keeping records. They should also feed back non-clinical information to enable employers to check that their control measures are working.

WHERE TO GET HELP

External advice

26   If you have no suitable in-house occupational health advice to draw on, call in outside help from a doctor or nurse trained in occupational medicine or occupational health nursing. For example, the Faculty of Occupational Medicine of the Royal College of Physicians has a graded system for the award of qualifications to doctors. The Diploma in Occupational Medicine (DOccMed) indicates that the holder, usually a general practitioner, has a basic level of competence across the whole field of occupational medicine and understands the practical and ethical considerations that apply at work. Associates of the Faculty hold a higher qualification (AFOM) and are usually in training to become specialists. Specialists will be Members of the Faculty (MFOM) or Fellows (FFOM) who should be able to deal with the full range and complexity of workplace problems.

27   Nurses should be registered with the United Kingdom Central Council for Nursing, Midwifery and Health Visiting (UKCC). They may have a degree, diploma or certificate in occupational health. You should ask the nurse for their Personal Identification Numbers (PIN) and confirm it (and their qualifications) with UKCC (see Appendix 2 for contact details).

28   You could also find out whether there are mobile clinics run by large local firms that you could hire to carry out health checks on your employees. When deciding, consider the cost, convenience, availability and expertise on offer.

29   Several professional bodies keep registers of competent practitioners. Your local HSE Employment Medical Advisory Service (EMAS) office will be able to help by providing general advice and will have details of doctors appointed to provide statutory medical surveillance under those regulations which require it. For more technical procedures, check whether the person is a member of the appropriate professional institution. Appendix 2 lists some of these; they may be able to direct you to someone suitable.

FREQUENCY AND LENGTH OF HEALTH SURVEILLANCE

30   Once you have decided to introduce health surveillance, continue it for at least as long as the individual is exposed to the risk. Increase the frequency of checks or examinations in borderline cases where it is not certain whether exposure might be causing harm. On the other hand, where it is clear that the risk has declined to a very low level, for example because of changing working practices or the introduction of new technology, you may relax the frequency of surveillance. In some cases, the health surveillance programme could be discontinued. Ask an occupational health professional for advice on this if you are in doubt.

31   Some regulations, for example those governing certain chemicals, lead or work in compressed air, expressly state the interval between examinations. Some also require employers to continue surveillance of people while still employed by them after exposure to the risk has stopped, to detect long-term disease, such as cancer, at an early stage.

Acting on the results

32   The real value from health surveillance will only be seen if you take appropriate action in response to the results and then check whether what you have done has worked. Where health surveillance shows that an employee's health is being affected by their work, take the following steps:

▶   Prevent further harm to the individual by reducing, or temporarily removing them from, exposure to the hazard. It may also be necessary to arrange for referral of the individual for further examination and/or treatment by a doctor with expertise in occupational health. Individuals shown to be particularly susceptible to illness or whose health has already been damaged, may need special protection.

- Re-examine your risk assessment to decide whether to take action to protect the rest of the workforce or to extend surveillance.

- Improve control measures if necessary, seeking the advice of specialists, for example occupational hygienists, as appropriate.

33   The results of health surveillance should be assessed by the person in charge of the programme. The results can be used in two ways. First, individual assessments should aim to improve the protection of the employees covered. You can achieve this by making sure that the person who conducts the health surveillance explains the significance of the results to the employee. This would include:

- explaining the state of the individual's health in relation to the health risk being tested for;

- discussing the correct use of PPE and the importance of using other control measures properly;

- explaining what happens next if any abnormality is detected; and

- stressing that individual medical details will not be released without the worker's written consent.

34   Second, by receiving an analysis of the health of groups of employees, you can gain an insight into how well your health risk control programme is working. Use the analysis to target your reduction, education and compliance practices more accurately. Such information should be suitably adapted to protect individuals' identities and be made available to safety or employee representatives.

REFERRAL ARRANGEMENTS AND MANAGING SPECIAL GROUPS

35   Where individuals are referred to an occupational health professional for further assessment, adequate information about the work the individual does should be given to the doctor or nurse to enable them to interpret their findings in relation to the employee's job. The assessment and treatment of these individuals is based on confidential nurse/patient or doctor/patient relationships. The health professional will recommend whether an individual remains fit to do

their usual job, whether alterations to current working arrangements are required or whether s/he should be moved to other work, perhaps under closer surveillance. Do not expect greater detail unless the employee has given their written permission for such information to be released to you.

36   It may be that, following a detailed medical assessment, the doctor or nurse recommends that the individual be moved to another job with less or no exposure to the health risk, explaining to you what type of job the individual can and cannot be expected to perform. In certain cases, you may have to conclude that you have no alternative but to terminate employment on health grounds. In handling such cases, act reasonably and remember that you have duties under employment law not to dismiss an employee unfairly or wrongfully and that the provisions of the Disability Discrimination Act 1995 might apply.

37   In particular, be aware that some groups of employees, for example pregnant workers, women of reproductive capacity or young workers may need special protection. See Appendix 1 for references to more detailed guidance.

38   Medical surveillance specifically under the Control of Lead at Work Regulations 1998, the Ionising Radiations Regulations 1985 and the COSHH Regulations 1999 can lead to a doctor declaring an employee unfit to work with the hazard concerned. In this case, you should seek to provide suitable other work, or suspend the employee from work (against which the employee has a right of appeal), until such time as the doctor certifies the employee fit for work. Detailed guidance on this is given in the Approved Codes of Practice to the Regulations.

Monitoring and evaluating the programme

39   Working with your occupational health adviser and involving your employees, regularly review how your health surveillance programme is working. Straightforward procedures, for example routine skin inspections, can be evaluated quite simply, based on whether there is any emerging evidence of ill health. In more complex schemes, such as where employees are exposed to a number of hazards that need different types of health surveillance, think about whether the range and frequency of the original procedures continue to meet your needs. New working techniques or better measurement methods may become available which affect the degree to which employees are put at risk of developing ill health.

Health records

40   Health surveillance programmes should include keeping a health record for each individual. These are important because they provide:

▶ an historical record of jobs involving exposure to substances or processes requiring health surveillance;

▶ a record of the outcome of previous health surveillance procedures (in terms of fitness for work, restrictions required etc); and

▶ information for HSE or local authority inspectors to show that health surveillance has been carried out.

41   Ensure that health records are completed routinely and systematically whenever individuals undergo health surveillance. A health record can be paper-based or held on computer and, as a minimum, should contain:

❑ Surname   ❑ Forenames   ❑ Sex

❑ Date of Birth   ❑ Permanent address   ❑ N.I. Number

❑ Date started present job

❑ an historical record of jobs involving exposure to hazards for which health surveillance is required during the current spell of employment;

❑ conclusions of health surveillance procedures and the date on which and by whom they were carried out. The conclusions should indicate whether the individual is fit to continue to work, including, where appropriate, the decisions of the doctor or nurse where medical assessments have taken place (but not clinical information), or the conclusions of other suitably qualified or responsible people.

42   Health records are different from clinical records in that they do not contain confidential clinical details and can therefore be kept securely with other confidential personnel records. Records which include medical information arising from clinical examination are held in confidence by the doctor, nurse or other occupational health professional and can only be released to you or anyone else with the written consent of the individual. The Access to Health Records Act 1990 allow employees a right to see and comment on their records.

Length of retention of health records

43   As a general rule, keep individual health records for those employees for as long as they are under health surveillance. Some regulations - COSHH and those for lead, asbestos, ionising radiations and compressed air - state that records should be retained for much longer (up to 50 years) as ill health effects might not emerge until a long time after exposure.

44   It is also good practice to offer individual employees a copy of their health records when they leave your employment. Employers about to cease to trade are obliged under COSHH 1999 to notify HSE and to offer to provide paper copies of employees' health records for safe keeping (the same action is recommended in guidance to the Control of Lead at Work Regulations 1998).

Implication of the Data Protection Directive

45   The Data Protection Act 1998 will come into force in the UK on 1 March 2000. It places new requirements on those who hold information on health and medical records. In particular, you will have to tell those on whom you hold records that a record is being kept, its purpose and that they have a right to see the information and correct it.

Other issues

Suitable facilities

46   Where health surveillance involves inspections, examinations, taking samples and making enquiries, make sure that there is adequate privacy for these to be carried out. Rooms should be clean, warm, airy and have suitable washing, lighting and (separate) toilet facilities.

RIDDOR reporting

47   Certain cases of disease are reportable to HSE or local authorities. These are listed in Schedule 3 to the Reporting of Injuries, Diseases and Dangerous Occurrences Regulations 1995 (see Appendix 1 for further reading). Some examples are occupational skin diseases; occupational asthma; and certain infections, occupational cancers and musculoskeletal disorders. The duty comes into effect where you receive a written statement from a registered medical practitioner (for example the employee's GP) stating that an employee suffers from one of the diseases and where the employee is currently doing a job involving a specific activity (also listed in the Schedule). Such statements can also act as a useful trigger for you to review how you manage health risks in your workplace.

HEALTH SURVEILLANCE

surveillance at work

Appendix 1: HSE publications:
Further reading on the health surveillance

CATEGORY	REFERENCES

SPECIFIC AGENTS

Noise

Health surveillance may be required under regulation 5 of the Management of Health and Safety at Work Regulations 1992 (*Management of health and safety at work* Approved Code of Practice L21 1992 HSE Books ISBN 0 11 886330 4)

SUPPORTING GUIDANCE

Health surveillance in noisy industries INDG193L 1995 HSE Books (Available in priced packs of 10, ISBN 0 7176 0933 2)

A guide to audiometric testing programmes MS 26 1995 HSE Books ISBN 0 7176 0942 1 provides more technical guidance

Vibration

Health surveillance may be required under regulation 5 of the Management of Health and Safety at Work Regulations 1992 (see reference under 'Noise')

SUPPORTING GUIDANCE

Hand-arm vibration HSG88 1994 HSE Books ISBN 0 7176 0743 7

Health risks from hand-arm vibration: Advice for employers INDG175(rev1) 1998 HSE Books (Available in priced packs of 10, ISBN 0 7176 1553 7)

Health risks from hand-arm vibration: Advice for employees and the self-employed INDG126(rev1) 1998 HSE Books (Available in priced packs of 10, ISBN 0 7176 1554 5)

Chemical and Biological Agents - general advice

Health surveillance may be required under regulation 11 of the Control of Substances Hazardous to Health Regulations 1999
(General COSHH ACOP and Carcinogens ACOP and Biological Agents ACOP L5 1999 HSE Books ISBN 0 7176 1670 3)

SUPPORTING GUIDANCE

Health surveillance under COSHH: Guidance for employers 1990 HSE Books ISBN 0 7176 0491 8

COSHH: The new brief guide for employers INDG136 1996 HSE Books (Available in priced packs of 10, ISBN 0 7176 1189 2)

Biological monitoring in the workplace: A guide to its practical application to chemical exposure HSG167 1997 HSE Books ISBN 0 7176 1279 1

Biological monitoring in the workplace: Information for employees on its application to chemical exposure INDG245 1997 HSE Books (Available in priced packs of 10, ISBN 0 7176 1450 6)

Any other guidance on work with biological agents prepared by HSC's Advisory Committee on Dangerous Pathogens

Chemical and

Biological Agents - specific hazards and ill health effects

Health surveillance and wood dust WIS33 1997 HSE Books

Toxic woods WIS30 1995 HSE Books

Silica CIS36 1993 HSE Books

Preventing asthma at work: How to control respiratory sensitisers L55 1994 HSE Books ISBN 0 7176 0661 9

Controlling health risks from rosin (colophony) based solder fluxes INDG249 1997 HSE Books (Available in priced packs of 10, ISBN 0 7176 1383 6)

Biological monitoring of workers exposed to organo- phosphates MS 17 1987 HSE Books ISBN 0 11 883951 9

Medical aspects of occupational asthma MS25 1998 HSE Books ISBN 0 7176 1547 2

Medical aspects of occupational skin disease MS24 1998 HSE Books ISBN 0 7176 1545 6

Guidance in the Environmental Hygiene (EH) series:

Cadmium: Health and safety precautions
EH1 1995 HSE Books ISBN 0 7176 0825 5

Chromium and its inorganic compounds: Health and safety precautions EH2 1998 HSE Books
ISBN 0 7176 1502 2

Beryllium: Health and safety precautions
EH13 1995 HSE Books ISBN 0 7176 0824 7

Isocyanates: Health hazards and precautionary measures EH16 1997 HSE Books ISBN 0 7176 1184 1

Mercury and its inorganic divalent compounds
EH17 1996 HSE Books ISBN 0 7176 1127 2

Ozone: Health hazards and precautionary measures
EH 38 1996 HSE Books ISBN 0 7176 1206 6

Dust: General principles of protection
EH44 1997 HSE Books ISBN 0 7176 1435 8

Respirable crystalline silica
EH59 1997 HSE Books ISBN 0 7176 1432 8

Nickel and its inorganic compounds: Health hazards and precautionary measures
EH60 1998 HSE Books ISBN 0 7176 1341 0

Vinyl chloride: Toxic hazards and precautions
EH63 1992 HSE Books ISBN 0 11 885730 4

Grain dust in maltings (maximum exposure limits)
EH67 1993 HSE Books ISBN 0 11 886357 6

Grain dust EH66 1998 HSE Books ISBN 0 7176 1535 9

Cobalt: Health and safety precautions
EH68 1995 HSE Books ISBN 0 7176 0823 9

Arsenic and its compounds: Health hazards and precautionary measures
EH73 1997 HSE Books ISBN 0 7176 1340 2

Lead

Medical Surveillance may be required under regulation 10 of the Control of Lead at Work Regulations 1998

SUPPORTING GUIDANCE

Control of lead at work Approved Code of Practice
COP2 1998 HSE Books ISBN 0 7176 1506 5

Asbestos

Medical examinations may be required under regulation 16 of the Control of Asbestos at Work Regulations 1987, as amended

SUPPORTING GUIDANCE

The control of asbestos at work. Control of Asbestos at Work Regulations 1987 Approved Code of Practice L27 1999 HSE Books ISBN 0 7176 1673 8

Asbestos: Medical guidance note MS13 1999 HSE Books ISBN 0 7176 2417 X

WORK IN COMPRESSED AIR

Medical surveillance may be required under regulation 10 of the Work in Compressed Air Regulations 1996

SUPPORTING GUIDANCE

A guide to the Work in Compressed Air Regulations 1996 L96 1996 HSE Books ISBN 0 7176 1120 5

WORK IN QUARRIES

Health and safety at quarries. Quarries Regulations 1999 Approved Code of Practice and guidance L118 1999 HSE Books ISBN 0 7176 2458 7

WORK IN MINES

The Mines Miscellaneous Health and Safety Provisions Regulations 1995

GUIDANCE IN SPECIFIC INDUSTRIES

Health surveillance programmes for employees exposed to metalworking fluids: Guidance for the responsible person INDG165 1994 HSE Books

Health surveillance in the foundry industry IACL104 1998 HSE Books

Health surveillance: A ceramics industry booklet IACL100 1996 HSE Books

Health surveillance requirements in electroplating EIS5 1998 HSE Books

COSHH and the woodworking industries WIS06(rev1) 1997 HSE Books

COSHH in agriculture AS28 1997 HSE Books

Grain dust in non-agricultural workplaces INDG140 1993 HSE Books

Occupational hygiene and health surveillance at industrial timber pre-treatment plants WIS29 1994 HSE Books

Isocyanates: Health surveillance in motor vehicle repair EIS18 1997 HSE Books

Reactive dyes: Safe handling in textile finishing TIS5 1997 HSE Books

Sheep dipping AS29(rev2) 1998 HSE Books

Veterinary medicines: Safe use by farmers and other animal handlers AS31 1998 HSE Books

A recipe for safety: Health and safety in the food industry TOP05(rev1) 1999 HSE Books

FITNESS FOR WORK ASSESSMENTS

Certificate of medical fitness to dive under regulation 11 of the Diving at Work Regulations 1997. The Regulations are accompanied by a leaflet: *Are you involved in a diving project?* INDG266 1998 HSE Books (Available in priced packs of 10, ISBN 0 7176 1529 4) and five Approved Codes of Practice:

Commercial diving projects offshore. Diving Regulations 1997 Approved Code of Practice LI03 1998 HSE Books ISBN 0 7176 1494 8

Commercial diving projects inland/inshore. Diving Regulations 1997 Approved Code of Practice LI04 1998 HSE Books ISBN 0 7176 1495 6

Recreational diving projects. Diving Regulations 1997 Approved Code of Practice LI05 1998 HSE Books ISBN 0 7176 1496 4

Media diving projects. Diving at Work Regulations 1997 Approved Code of Practice LI06 1998 HSE Books ISBN 0 7176 1497 2

Scientific and archaeological diving projects. Diving Regulations 1997 Approved Code of Practice LI07 1998 HSE Books ISBN 0 7176 1498 0

Fitness to work medical surveillance under regulation 16 of the Ionising Radiations Regulations 1985 (under review) and guidance, *The protection of persons against ionising radiation arising from any work activity* Approved Code of Practice L58 1994 HSE Books ISBN 0 7176 0508 6

OTHER USEFUL
GUIDANCE

Successful health and safety management
HSG65 1997 HSE Books ISBN 0 7176 1276 7

Managing health and safety: Five steps to success
INDG275 1998 HSE Books

Five steps to risk assessment
INDG163 1998 HSE Books (Available in priced packs
of 10, ISBN 0 7176 1565 0)

Health risk management
HSG137 1995 HSE Books ISBN 0 7176 0905 7

Selecting a health and safety consultancy
INDG133 1992 HSE Books

Safety representatives and safety committees
L87 1998 HSE Books ISBN 0 7176 1220 1

*Consulting employees on health and safety: A guide to
the law* INDG232 1996 HSE Books (Available in
priced packs of 10, ISBN 0 7176 1615 0)

Young people at work: A guide for employers
HSG165 1997 HSE Books ISBN 0 7176 1285 6

*New and expectant mothers at work: A guide for
employers*
HSG122 1998 HSE Books ISBN 0 7176 0826 3

REPORTING CASES
OF DISEASE

*A guide to the Reporting Of Injuries, Diseases and
Dangerous Occurrences Regulations 1995*
L73 1996 HSE Books ISBN 0 7176 1012 8

RIDDOR explained
HSE 31 1996 HSE Books (Available in priced packs
of 10, ISBN 0 7176 2441 2)

RIDDOR: Information for doctors
HSE 32 1996 HSE Books

HSE has also agreed various sector-specific guidance which has been published
by trade associations.

While every effort has been made to ensure the accuracy of the references listed
in this publication, their future availability cannot be guaranteed.

Appendix 2: Where to get help

Suppliers of equipment and substances or trade associations often provide information on specific health risks. This will help you determine whether health surveillance is appropriate. Occupational health advisers can help you apply this information to your own activities. You may be able to tap into local group occupational health services or independent consultants, for example. Other sources of advice could come from employer organisations and local Chambers of Commerce.

HSE EMAS addresses

HSE has a network of local offices, many of which have medical and nursing specialists who can provide advice on occupational health. Telephone HSE's InfoLine on 0541 545500 who will be able to put you through to someone who can help you.

Professional institutions

A number of prominent professional institutions could also give you information:

The Faculty of Occupational Medicine
6 St Andrew's Place
Regents Park
London
NW1 4LB
Tel: 0171 317 5890
E-mail: fom@compuserve.com

British Safety Council
70 Chancellor's Rd
London W6 9RS
Tel: 0181 741 1231
E-mail:
bscl@mail.britishsafetycouncil.co.uk

Society of Occupational Medicine
6 St Andrew's Place
Regents Park
London
NW1 4LB
Tel: 0171 486 2641
E-mail:
societyoccmed@compuserve.com

Ergonomics Society
Devonshire House
Devonshire Square
Loughborough
Leics LE11 3DW
Tel: 01509 234904
E-mail: ergsoc@ergonomics.org.uk

Society of Occupational Health
Nursing
The Royal College of Nursing
20 Cavendish Square
London W1M 0AB
Tel: 0171 409 3333

Royal Society for the Prevention of
Accidents
Edgbaston Park
353 Bristol Rd
Birmingham B5 7ST
Tel: 0121 248 2000
E-mail: help@rospa.com

Institute of Occupational Safety and
Health (IOSH)
The Grange
Highfield Drive
Wigston
Leicester LE18 1NN
Tel: 0116 257 3100
E-mail: comms@iosh.co.uk

United Kingdom Central Council for
Nursing, Midwifery and Health
Visiting
23 Portland Place
London W1N 3JT
Tel: 0171 637 7181
E-mail: advice@ukcc.org.uk

British Occupational Hygiene Society
(BOHS)
Suite 2
Georgian House
Great Northern Rd
Derby DE1 1LT
Tel: 01332 298101
E-mail: bohs@compuserve.com

British Institute of Occupational
Hygienists (BIOH)
Suite 2
Georgian House
Great Northern Rd
Derby DE1 1LT
Tel: 01332 298087
E-mail: bioh@compuserve.com

Institute of Acoustics
Agricultural House
5 Holywell Hill
St Albans AL1 1EU
Tel: 01727 848195
E-mail: acoustics@clus1.ulcc.ac.uk

Glossary of terms

Health surveillance is a process involving a range of techniques used to detect early signs of work-related ill health among workers exposed to certain health risks; and subsequently acting on the results.

Medical surveillance is health surveillance requiring the specific skills and expertise of a doctor, which may include clinical examinations.

Medical/clinical examinations are those carried out by a health professional and are subject to ethical codes ensuring confidentiality of information.

Baseline health assessments involve a range of techniques used at the pre-assignment stage to determine a worker's health status in relation to the hazards they are likely to be exposed to at work.

Fitness for work assessments are specific checks to assess whether an individual is fit to undertake the work they will be doing without unacceptable risk to themselves or to others.

Health monitoring is a generic term covering the full range of techniques - statutory and non-statutory - to monitor the health of individuals during their employment.

Signs and symptoms of disease. *Signs* are objective evidence of ill health (ie what a doctor might find on a medical examination). *Symptoms* are subjective indicators of ill health (ie what the sufferer experiences, for example a cough or shortness of breath).

Health records are historical records. They provide information about an individual's job, involving exposure to substances or processes requiring health surveillance and, where relevant, the conclusions of the person undertaking health surveillance. They may be kept securely with other confidential personnel records.

Clinical medical records include confidential medical information on an individual held by a health professional.

Printed and published by the Health and Safety Executive   10/99   C120